DOPAMINE BLUNDER

lori cayer

DOPAMINE BLUNDER

TIGHTROPE BOOKS

Tightrope Books
#207-2 College Street,
Toronto Ontario, Canada M5G 1K3
tightropebooks.com
bookinfo@tightropebooks.com

EDITOR: Laura Lush
COPYEDITOR: Deanna Janovski
COVER DESIGN: Deanna Janovski
LAYOUT DESIGN: David Jang

Produced with the assistance of the Canada Council for the Arts and the Ontario Arts Council.

Library and Archives Canada Cataloguing in Publication

Cayer, Lori, author
        Dopamine blunder / Lori Cayer.

Poems.
ISBN 978-1-988040-05-9 (paperback)

        I. Title.

PS8605.A94D66 2016   C811'.6   C2016-901188-7

Well-being is attained little by little,
and nevertheless is no little thing itself.
Zeno of Elea

If you want to be happy, be.
Leo Tolstoy

CONTENTS

Page Not Found

how do you know if you're happy
if you're not   how do you

if everything strikes you   literally
and you worry   and twirl
upon the economics of happiness
      entitlement enters   correlates strongly

a lot of it, it's true   you can buy
textiles, engorged baubles, architecture

the diminishment of return
not linear   but logarithmic

you seem to know it best   when you smooth
your feet into whatever you call bed

turn a few pages before tripping
toward   the riparian ridge   between risking it
and falling asleep

How Stoics Are Happy

<

if a feeling is only a feeling, and not a state of affairs, such as your slings
and arrows argue, then
you are an oily wall of letting be, a solid case for amnesia, your spiny
regrets, all that injured business still alive in the locked-down past

<

if a feeling is a neuro-cognitive event, unspirited, only for rent, then
you are a cold shoulder turned, an animal purged of urges
for {heart/heart}, sternums touching, hopeful primate prisoners
each on their side of the ventral/ventral wall

<

if you must slough the untenable, that shoulder a sail-bone
puncturing a way away, then so too love
must be dropped behind like a hair cut, equal for equal
deny wonder, deny colours oxygenating themselves into your cells

<

if you call it as it is, your heart muscle hibernating—then electricity—then
myelination is all that holds your arms wide apart under the sun, takes
a picture of the back of your eye, the light circle
where blind spots converge, the sun still shining there, wanting you

Heresy of Invisible Things

a)
start or end with a string
                    of muse
the muse of the theory
of the very small, so

small as to say
invisible
give to nothing
a set of names

say quantum say mechanics
the arcing brain vaults
surmise
their exquisite bullshit

explain nothing
explain vast
and lo
nothing is made real

b)
take   time
and disabuse it of itself

call it linear, call it explosive
warped or plied in laminations

my concurrent selves folding
laundry, etc.

call it the
one
drum
beat of now

c)
space
is the space between spaces

impossible objects hurl, make recordable noise
an absence of light we will call dark

has all the properties of nothing
whatsoever

which we will call matter
yarned into fabric of visual aid

maybe string and time invisibly
we need this naming

d)
money   an idea of numbers
there is no room big enough
if each

number
were an object of matter, a coin stamped

your poverty and mine merely ink
we'll still die

no paper falsely effaced
using only imagination, print as needed

your wealth, your asset relief
you'll still die

fundamental notions
such as these
belong to our nature

e)
dark material of computer's
deep magic
dark magic of mathematics

solve for, decode for
muse, elucidate the particles
of energy, invisible bubbles

of actual nothing
haloed around heads
each a moment

greater or lesser than

f)
and god came burgeoning

an equation of weather

and an oversized brain

god came from fire

the dead one loved

the sky impossibly lit by night:

from there god came burgeoning

Human Development Index

$$\text{HDI} =$$

$$\tfrac{1}{3} \text{ (life expectancy index)}$$
$$+$$
$$\tfrac{1}{3} \text{ (education index)}$$
$$+$$
$$\tfrac{1}{3} \text{ (GDP index)}$$

Consolation of Philosophy

the tumour was not dug in, the country only maimed
its name mis-remembered in a breath, the plane did not crash
wide open in this trajectory

today death did not come along like a cliché rattling its rickety
bike down jay-walk road, like
something red collapsed between the teeth

we count our ragged blessings relative to mass extinction
when the pinholes are calibrated to the south
when the spark of hunger comes we rise, hypoxic and alive

Caritas

out there in the green admonishment   a tribe
still living its referent-beliefs
a throwback, an empirical irony
asked how happy—given of course—a scale
please, with a pencil
select from: sad to enlightened
select level of tolerance: putrid to sacred
how striven   how flourished versus
     not

when they have no word for happy
they answer: *pods, sing, paint* or *spear*
draw the question without word—where
the strange phenomena of their soul   the inner
work to meet it   test of all other rules
that do not obey normal principles

they reply: *smoke, vines, hunger* and *fed*
     is and now
caritas   (if they want elusive)
(one of our words)

Hierarchy of Needs: *Telegrams from the Interior*

please advise

at the roots of bliss the hair is fine
and damp—like vernix, like mycorrhiza

envisioned moments of extraordinary wellness
(as if I could take them up)

this week alone, fall's leaves, green grass
and fresh snow, each acting as if—

functional harmony, punctual threnody
practice of virtue against your lesser self

behind the throat, from ear membrane to
butterfly-bundle of pelvis, a thumping garden hose

I'm still afraid, characterized by various factors
a mix of finally and what next

stop

Cure for the Now

the chances of us writing something backwards
increases phonetically when light hits us
       from behind, shows us the shape
of the story but not the words
our ratio of fulfilled desires (to total desires)
we must respond with hope, a dialectical translation
best done with our eyes closed, to bring
something transcended out from the bush
            in any case we keep on
our ends
inclusive of our means
       an entity of blur and eardrum vibrato
that shifts as one animal into the trees

Happy Planet Index

HPI (subjective life satisfaction)
+
(life expectancy at birth)
+
(ecological footprint per capita)
/3

Acts of Confiscation

I commit new crimes   to push
down the line   the unbearable ones
drop them off the conveyor
into ether or
the shine-deficient space
 left between   stars

you, oh   you
rescue Rez dogs
work overseas
with the starved, look good
on the resumé, on the passport
your goodness makes you
fairly crack
like a sung wineglass
like the sun
in pieces on water

I'm going in the red   direction
commit acts the size of ( )   always
some hole with fallen edges
a same-shaped desire waiting to fill it
handing out unexecuted synonyms   I do
I want back those
years, those years

Now Tulip

last year's lost poem was sad and angry
it described winter still shrieking in spring—bookended—
both equinoxes under snow

desolation house, every day trapped
chew-your-own-foot-off kind of trap
the dog, forsaken, draped his body for viewing

[one] day I rose up, booted and gloved, pretended
a striding love of snow—dirty, pitted, elderly kind of snow
and rickety ice beneath—then

green fingers exhuming, patch of dirt
orange fist of flesh petalling awake
fully opened: the animal eye of tulip

Havana, Street Dogs

amidst buildings opulently decaying, stores empty of wares
this city of dogs—so homeless—yet so healthy on scrap
in-bred islanders, all cousins of mutt
inhabiting the edges   the edges
inches from the river-of-walking-feet
you turn from tourist to thwarted missionary
your petting hands would gather up
their lives, in acts of wire and love

perfect socialists, they get part of what they need
and must need no more
dogs, that when you speak to them
do not look for the source of the voice
do not hear their mother in that pure calling

Havana, Pet Shop

on the cobblestones, cages stacked—a market stall
with walls of air
For Sale: small iterations
heartbeats bouquet-gathered into
a travelling show of wanting
who would buy a dog or carry home a bird?
when both are city-abundant
for free, beseeching

skirt your way around it
try to unsee these browns and browns of eyes
unfeel how desire moves in captivity
a pet shop showing something
of the animal in and the animal
out

The World Happiness Report

/scale running 0 to 10/6 key variables explain ¾ variation/annual/
population-weighted average score/over time/among countries/

1. real GDP per capita

2. healthy life expectancy

3. having someone to count on

4. perceived freedom to make life choices

5. freedom from corruption

6. generosity

Travelling without Moving

The last line always comes first, how oddly and often
words group or branch off, like paper clips, spoons, etc.

it relaxes me to sort and rearrange, I'm pretty sure it was me
in the cupboards and boxes, O lost poem I wrote

when I'm dead they shall not discover me
a hoarder of anything but stones and feathers

what a laugh when I open a drawer, what prankster moved these things

I am afraid for my furled brain, call my self Mrs. Alzheimer
what she knew of forgetting, I started to write something—

Terror Management Theory: The Paradox of Guidance

your meaningful life of barn raising, church
many hands around the dinner table; postpone

the true gift of happiness with your clear and moral
reason, oily duck feathers shedding what is futile

but which continues to rain down—your one book both
carrot and stick, coherence of aims knitting wants with needs

finding work, daily work, work of each day, a blessing day and day
the harp inside the piano

the picture inherent in the puzzle, guiding you
in fitting together its pieces—a kind of daylight in the mind

A Problem of Subjective Evaluation

is it plausible to call a satisfied depressive happy?
a happy agnostic satisfied? what if this is you?

                                        asking

the connection between preference satisfaction and life
satisfaction is substantially arbitrary.

                              eggplant or figs

eggplant or hunger   figs or fucking
the standards in use
at a given time affect the nature of a definition of a theory

you will examine happiness as an ethical theory
                              a relative
affective state

with a blank vigour that rankles, some of you will tend
the harvest   water wand in hand   tend also
                                        episodically

your bodies—maul them gently under like earth
others of you will measure your goals
		both tangible and realized

constructs based on judgement theory, happiness
and its cognates
			in ordinary language:

boredom		with moments of elation		misplacement
of stars
		semantic drift

there are real things at stake
as in supported		as in risk
it's the juxtaposition of findings that will ruin everything

Leonard Nimoy Dies

but how long   this grammatical act without
end
he dies
          taking his usual   aeons
shifting
his temporal degeneration   to black   and
white
          headline keeps him   infinitely here
          he dies
and continues   to do so
          a night slippage we would
          expect
his marrow and
          robes   suspended

Happiness Economics

$$W_{it} = \alpha + \beta x_{it} + \varepsilon_{it}.$$

W is the reported well-being of individual i at time t

x is a vector of known variables (socio-demographic and socioeconomic characteristics)

Both Blackened Ends of Day: Telegrams from the Exterior

please advise

to give air to the skinned off branch
itself, more like me now

the crow lives among us in cities
sharp, ringing steps on orders

my dad came back from hunting
familiar, failure of recognition

how the rain just comes and runs through
water-like, feather-like

any boots but mine
because I don't stand on roads outside of cities

the frozen cat curled, in the dirt corner
the winter farm not caring

It takes over fast, the earth, and its proclivities
an idea like an explosion in space

stop

Sagittarius A* Star

like an object in space, he passes me, an averted angle
all my joy injures him, dumb happiness for nothing
his gravity pulls it all down, an unbalanced hurling
debris field of dead-heavy stones, blast-melted crystals and iron
my orbit nearly stationary (as)

as that black hole, the big one you don't know about
scribbling itself silly with stars, gas giants in their unkempt
orbits like flies around the head
doughnut centred, it invisibles itself into dark constancy
edges pouring inward, a sucking chest wound in the milky way

that's more what it's like   my hands
trying sleights of happiness
joyful things pulled forth in bursts of colour
                        *Sagittarius A**
                          * = star
the flat middle eye
it's not known when, but in some number eons
it will all be sucked in and gone

Utilitarianism: As Written by Cat

0n+.0n+.0n+.0n+.0n+
0n+.0n+.0n+.0n+.0n+.0n+.0n+.0n
.0n+.0n+.0n+.0n+.0n+.0n+
.0n+.0n+.0n+.0n+.0n+.0n+.0n+.0n+.0n+

.0n+.0n+.0n+.0n+.0n+.0n+.0n+.0n+
0n+.0n+.0n+.0n+.0n+.0n+
+.0n+.0n+.0n+.0n+.0n+.+.0n+.0n+.0n
n+.0n

0n+.0n+.0n+.0n+.0n+.0n+0n+.0
.0n+.0n+.0n+.0n+.0n+.0n+
n+.0n
.0n+.0n+.0n+.0n+.0n+.0n+.0n+.0n+.0n+

.0n+.0n+.0n+.0n+.0n+.0n+.0n+.0n+
+.0n+.0n+.0n+.0n+.0n+.0n+.0n+.0n+.0n+.0n+.0n+

Hitchhiking to Scotland

the day you were born I was hitchhiking to Scotland
(everyone I met said they'd known the Beatles before
they were famous) I'm sorry I was that young and disbelieving
I didn't know it was your birth[day]

or how my years and your years would turn me mean
and you addicted (I'm sorry I missed the entrance to your
pain, how burrowed and trenched, but you sure
faked that loud happy goodness

we loved) I'm sorry I was hitchhiking on your birth[day]
your death[day]—the day you decided
I worked my desk and walked the dog and watched tv
nothing called me   I wasn't waiting   everything was fine

Happiness =

Happiness = P + (5xE) + (3xH)

P: Personal characteristics, including outlook on life, adaptability and resilience.

H: Higher order needs, including self-esteem, expectations, ambitions and sense of humour.

E: Existence, relates to health, financial stability and friendships.

Crying: Discussing Its Critical Steps

Abstract

a sort of taboo still holds
to withhold or delay crying
    is
a protest left to the helpless
the helplessness hypothesis
    is
speculative in nature
such a collapse and surrender and so
    on
    this
sounds convincing after all
something has been done warded
    off
some offering has been given
sealing a return to ordinary

Introduction

we suggest   and will try to show   coginitive causes
like
the vastness of the sea, say
people cry
in a great variety   (in front of some reason)
not
surprisingly   grouping crying under categories—
elation dejection anguish   the various displays
either expected
or
some sights   unexpected

Methods

crying can be a means   can occur
in all
the crying contexts   the final overt step
of an
internal and unobservable process
pointing to attempts   the situation
and the
particular catharsis   consists
in the
mitigation of   self-repudiation, incapability
resistance the key

Results

we have
addressed the possible
crying-for-joy is very likely, would be   congruent
religious—aesthetic—empathic, etc.
we have also
considered things one would like to hold, reflect
one feels there is still room
of course
for a message of appeasement, a happy ending

Discussion

we have described the process
in fact—as just remarked—for instance
weeping, sobbing watery eyes
both
are signs   favouring awareness
crying can also imply so few data
in turn
induces flowchart levels of intensity, see fig. 1
each class of crying   (those features which qualify)
would
deserve a work of its own   failure can be more less
discouraging,   depending

Concluding Remarks

do not rule out the possibility
crying favours   crying expresses   discouragement
but
together with those features
ingredients have been added to the
core
defensive strategies implied   using different targets
the uses of crying are manifold
sometimes
surrender is premature   stemming
from
inability to recognize oneself
trying to remedy
      and the matter can be closed

Where-to-Be-Born Index

Material well-being as measured by GDP per capita

+

Life expectancy at birth

+

Quality of family life based primarily on divorce rates

+

State of political freedoms

+

Job security

+

Climate

+

Personal physical security ratings

+

Quality of community life

+

Governance

+

Gender equality

Ambulance

headful of broken windows
knees and a laundry bag of elbows
    lifted out of the road_sky
rocked awake
cracked stars envisioned,   then rocking
in a rocking bed
    i just told you
the ordinary world went wrap-around
fracture, then i
into   without   memory
through pavement_sky   fell
the small_small world
of pavement befalling me
yesterday, the chances of this
exactly the same   as
this happens sometimes
today
today, it's just some kind of normal

Memories of Dystopian Home

it's taken till this cataract of evening to get it all
so wrong, this room full of memorabilia
serial longings and incompletions
to which I have attempted to apply paint
or turn back like watches

I was developing my hypothesis about that stupid
desiderata when I saw you arriving with all your
disappointments, having also confused what is desired
with what is desirable   and together
settling down to watch the late news

Eudemonia

you're so present tense
your sloughed skin cells carried
seven and seven years down the river

dispersed   that you might not be remade
accidentally, in a neighbouring country
of your own dna sludge
your erstwhile selves

your head always a room
refreshingly swept
where every tortured thing you've given up
suspends   wrapped in air

your annoying preference for the is
of what is
working your desire   your desire
satisfaction theory

you are very well   subjectively
a sheer wash of medium rosy pink
the rewarding nature of flow

Self-Portrait, Wicker Chair

just like this: widest awake and in the perfect
of a summer morning
breeze optional, sun unconditional

not hit by or stricken with
no last ticket to anywhere I've always wanted
but maybe a gin and tonic, all flowers and sap

let it go delving for a core sample
long strata of confinement listing
all my figments and true things

like this, closing my eyes to promising
blue holes of sky availing themselves
between clouds, a soft

clickable fade to black
an act of such nothing can only happen once
everything opening unbearably wider

Light Trespass

you emerge from a dream in damp confusion, still hauling up
your heavy net full of wreckage, all china and iron and chairs

people you don't even know, to sort from aggregates to elements
an ether-fracted story spun and unspinning between surface-foam and air

the impossible problem of clarity, a factored leap, the emptying
of cramped hands, an open practice of waking for its own sake

your unfinished dinner below, companions with their mouths
all bubble waiting for what you were about to say

Positive and Negative Affect Schedule (PANAS)

State how you've felt in the last week, with 1 being Very slightly or Not at all and 5 being Quite a bit or Extremely.

POSITIVE		NEGATIVE	
Interested	_____	Irritable	_____
Distressed	_____	Alert	_____
Excited	_____	Ashamed	_____
Upset	_____	Inspired	_____
Strong	_____	Nervous	_____
Guilty	_____	Determined	_____
Scared	_____	Attentive	_____
Hostile	_____	Jittery	_____
Enthusiastic	_____	Active	_____
Proud	_____	Afraid	_____

Paradox of Hedonism

where the little dogs run, the Italian marble is dander-dusted
stamens rain down from aging bouquets

the pool is a lovely shape though tainted by the
neighbour's spyglass—motes float, leaves—slime

gets under elastic and itches. I should have
a better pool, perhaps those orange gilded fishes

the damn books are dusty if you look at the tops
that bitch neighbour, so Hollywood, so stretched

my lot in this life

I should have a housekeeper, at least
disappointment is dirty and has so many rooms
I wipe one thing and another, but still it looks

like someone lives here

All I Have

interior of city, its two seasons: *Hate* and *Forgiveness*
Buildings, roads, things, the people amongst   ghost coloured

gravel sieves the snow, eight months indoors magnifies

sun pretends wide over frozen absence

I am sub   total, my skin gone irrational, not even birds   out
In the walls the thinnest sound, hiatus of sleep, its complicated nest

dirty lady fingernailing tiny seeds   into
placing under lights   just in case

I was packed to leave for any other poverty
greater than or less   than

when *Forgiveness* got here, acting like it was nothing
All temperate, cascading her arms full   of birds

fine,   but this is the last time I fall,   her
offering green like a brief and dangled afterthought

View from the Halfway Point

normal helps
the us or we of it   dislodges
the domestic from its normative articulations
we could live worse, with more art

more words tending away from our singular hands
our rhetorical happenings sent
from the gift economy, received at the door like
online orders

our cohorts will fail, or not
at happiness, at keeping the bathroom clean
or burn us down with their successes
it will all become a poor approximation of memory

the occasion of this interview, at this speed
is syntactically alarming, decisions
derived from dream material, thin grasps of grace
                              but normal helps, don't you find?

Second Wind

his neural event opens one eye all the way
obliterating the blue iris, it lets in all
available light

turning nocturnal, the white cat is getting ready
to go   or come, medically, part way
back

head tips sideways, locks   owlish
circuitry bears him to the left, turns him in
awkward circles

fur turning to imagined snowy feather, he scans
in a field of broken light,   a broken field
for that hand, that hand

holding down the earth's question, how
such a departure can be already   and also
not quite yet

suddenly, it seems,   mice
skittering away, his blue eye following
this won't make sense, for some time to come

Momentary Subjective Well-Being

$$\text{Happiness}(t) =$$
$$w0 + w1\sum j =$$
$$1t\,\gamma\,t - CRj + w2\sum j =$$
$$1t\gamma t - jEVj + w3\sum j =$$
$$1t\gamma t - jRPEj$$

Erasing the {music} Garden

<
sky teeters   {blue {,} light}   among a remnant circle
snow-stitched
crows
disinherit   the   mundane

hanging from bowed limbs
stringy throng   corolla
of Bach of glitter and shadow
side   by   side

<
peeling shadows   the garden
like music
{blue {-} grey}
tenor of dusk
    holding court : blazing {orange}
Bach   floating
in
the
falling
{yellow}
pouring
with
rain

<

sky {grey} as war torrents
and drum

glass-held
courting the long day

real life falling
particles
dusk
setting   {pink} through
words

<

limb of wind   calling   calling

          standing still
twilight chasing stillness
                    moonlit   clinging

small chambers
                    break the sky
          a million pinches
of shadow

<

walk through switch
                    grass   arms deciduous

over dry heave of pier   lungs skirt
the arc of round
{
black} notes down-curved

to {cobalt} sky

<

      curving as lyre
    wind-dragged
           under
listen   down
           through
hear   wingrush
          departing
                      {black}}}}}}}}}} horizon
wind-trebled note

>

          {pink} remnants
of
cold

listen to trees
          cymbal across snow

a note on your hands
        your miracle

Gross National Happiness

value =
index function/total average per capita/measures

Economic **Wellness**, Environmental **Wellness**, Physical **Wellness**,
Mental **Wellness**, Workplace **Wellness**, Social **Wellness**, Political **Wellness**

Refusal Conversion

search for love from your chair
cast for dropped traces, wiki-sexual, your place
in a place which does not, for all intents, exist

freefloat there (everyone does) find each other
joyful, privacies clearly stated, your own face
from different angles, midstream, mouth ajar

honest enough, in this squared light, nothing tells
the truth, you are re-questing, souls made showy
and complex, as heaven must be, if heaven were

also built by personal deposits, the end of practical
obscurity, admit you want it, this way, at night
look at, and into
save yourself—save as—send

On Fire at the Wedding

it sure was an anecdote, how it started
you so innocently not   yet married to me
standing next to our friend, married for ages
when someone else passes you their new new baby
and   just then   the wedding photographer
snap/snaps you into a forever family

one degree of blurred, I made my way to the dessert
table, where the long   fringes of my sleeve dipped
lightly into an anecdote
into a candle nestled amongst   how my arm
like a bouquet flying up
lit orange   some-hundred people not seeing

not seeing me, on fire   agog
my polyesters a flash mob flaring
then split/gone like   never been
like I,   like I had never been
seen pounding out flames
forwardly walking back
to our table, with not even smoke   trailing

Eve Song

the garden is blooming and ravelling the way it does
my husband hawking and showing his fruit at market

he aims to please, never leaving socks around, etc.
his unlined ease, a boyish vessel

man, it irks me, my so-called serenity pulled through
in diminishing threads, fruition furrowing

will this be all, then?   find sharp objects
to etch the walls, grind and press paint from blue stone?

I can't make a sufficient crime out of this
a grave smirk has been tightening my smile

he turns me
on my axis like a red orb

Flash Reduction

if   I find a diamond on the floor its size is
immediately big or small   depending
a calving off of carat lost from its claw
      a light from the sun falls   *a sun fall*

if   somewoman is saddened   her gaping mouth
a cawing ring clawing   is she diminished or am I
enhanced   fit to bind and be bound
      afflicted with purity   *buoyancy*   *ricochet*

if   no-one witnessed its unsubtle way to the puddle
of my palm   is it
a dominant form   a vestigial abstraction
      light-scissor   *bright fossil*   *a hole of gravity?*

if   you and I don't care   *skin-held*   *indivisible*
if   the diamond doesn't care   *organ of light-carve*
it waits at our house for its meaning
      quicksilver   *monstrous embryo*

still   by way of standard declaration
ephemeral made narrative   made temporal   *lithic*
      flinted   *imperfect fluid*
it's what I've got

Eight Domains of the Canadian Index of Wellbeing

CommunityVitalityDemocraticEngagementEducationEnvironment
HealthyPopulationsLeisureCultureLivingStandardsTimeUse

Small Misses, Nearly Caught

<

lost   lost
your[::] baby
in the MASSIVE blue MASSIVE blue, [your] catastrophic genes
                                                dreams
not so much blue screen of death but pictures
of little flowers
indicators the connectome works
beneath
screen capture   the moment
you   [are become]
eternally lonely

<

just thought I'd give [you] a quick
strangest dream
from the stormblue room
about [you :: us]
same as
not so much care > as expectation
not so much debt > as scar tissue
pulling   stitches between then and the
new   blue now, [my] long
life since, [one of us]   waiver
hang up, just hang up

<

salvage lines
ground-layer lichens, feathermosses and vascular plants
bitter/BLUE chain
one time I [::] was crazy and violently sad
hostile witness
[your]   eyes were
the colour of outside
blue-jay blue   hazing   into white
they left open the lid::hinge squawk
fractal unfold
          there's night rising   rearview
    the   windshield still driving into day

Human Poverty Index

HPI =

      : Probability at birth of not surviving to age 60 (times 100)

      : Adults lacking functional literacy skills

      : Population below income poverty line (50% of median
        adjusted household disposable income)

      : Rate of long-term unemployment (lasting 12 months or more)

      : 3

Declensions of Altruistic Giving

<
you don't even try to fight it   >urge
    >urge to donate your   self
 (altruism described as a sickness
give to the dying, your maximum of body parts

<
despair   you must harbour the rest
    softboil of brain, >cut-out shape
    of heart   sadly cannot be disposed
or the giver will be   gone

<
instead (it has to hurt
has to   cut in
to feel your goodness, really feel it
hole the hand went in   let it heal (appeal

<
till the give-imperative comes again
delaminating
your troubled assets   they come off thin
(sheen like mica   like fascia

<
so few parts to give, yet the urge >extremis
>plies (compiles (compounds
care must be under   taken
(transplant (transaction

<

if you kill the host, the first thing they will ask for
will be   your eyes)
needed within the hour
for another blind head

your eyes)
that you may see again

Next to the Wreckage of the World

your circumstantial beliefs carry you
through the right now of your now
gambling your last
for the certainty of success
fog of poverty long gone

you are money trap now, sticky web
slight electrical cling in the air
attracting dollar signs
in your world, cash poor is character poor
it has a smell

wherever you are, that mother you had
father you didn't, your own private mandala
starbursting to perfect infinite destination
the pain of wanting will never
sand to smoothness, such ghosts

Nematic Onscreen Gamine/16 Anagrams for MRI/

I'm fine inside: starboard aiming
of eardrum, ensnares sound, enacts an image: me as shavings
of light, emit overlays of molecule music
galactic pod going somewhere for years: gametic, manic

Is this dead? this blood/humming dissonance
magnets like truck tires, I pass through braking, beseeching, body
drummed: narcose, cellular
chaotic church organ decibled all the way to aortic groan

how can sonance be: a cylindrical thinking thing
drawing my variances
like god—might be a thing—acerose, passing through
in loose parallel lines, not leaving traces but taking

them: mantic and animate
grinding circular, picking through the sound garbage
scanner plainly hidden inside resonance
Oh wow I am a machine   /take my picture/

Set-Point Theory

true calm may be re-set by {shinrin-yoku}
forest bathing
the deep study
of taking a walk in the woods
save the life you can save

your happiness{es} assessed, each to their own domains
: work, family, romantic love
          etc.
: sampled randomly {variously objected}
: finally averaged, applied a value
: measured longitudinally
: overcoming craving in all forms

this is your antidote for death from overwork {{karōshi}}
a set of purposes   typically human
in response to
          the breath of
          the woods
Chamaecyparis obtusa {} stem oil
hinoki cypress   vaporized

The Popsicle Index

(percentage of people)
(who believe a child in their community)
(can safely leave home)
(buy a popsicle)
(and safely return)

Touch Like Blindness

wasps do it in the fall, arriving like I am sun
they taste my skin, touch their way

along without lifting   five:
like fingers scribbling

the hard part is waiting them out, nerves
a balloon of white light and punctuation

hold still, they write
this shouldn't hurt

Close Throat

usually fire to fire   strung

circling the snake   through the night

sutured   house was shattered
       screw
       through
       the
       floor
garments stitched to bodies   cinch

instances of choking   various sums

furtive operations   given to strange strange

paper   fluttered up   flashed over

           these, of course

         silence

Midst

mid-traumatic stress, pre-disorder
I found I was far from myself
on the phone in an old city
having stepped into a lilac tree
because it was raining
and words were coming and pedestrians
were blearing by
this poor umbrella a wet embrace

once I just was—some kid who thought
post was a letter, stress held up bridges
trauma was not an environment
and our lilac tree was an instrument into which
strings I stepped, a hollow my size
like it was a telephone booth, like I hoped for a beam
a dressing room to gather me into a garment
of matter

Dirt Clinic

if I am found in the woods
                    with my diagnosis
a little drunk, a lot overdosed
                    then leave me:
sleeping in my big sweater, cooling in my skirl of leaf litter

sure, if I ponder the rocks bridges ovens of poets before me
                    feel free:
help with your helping, talk my gazing ball clear, insist your
cocktails and theories
I'm in love as the next person, with hope and its irradiated secrets

          if I miss my moment   forgetforgetforget   to step
          forward
          and the train
                    leaves without me:
I will need you, to do the something that should be done
or the nothing   till I've hungered away or overdrifted
sweetly

if my subjective pain, my objective terminus is such
                    unplug me:
etc. pass the electric smoothie, end this
doctoring of the dead before the dead is me
having come this far with me
a ceremony in and of itself
today is a long time to waste

ABOUT THE AUTHOR

Lori Cayer is the author of two volumes of poetry:
Stealing Mercury and *Attenuations of Force*. She is a former
co-editor for *Contemporary Verse 2* and is co-founder of the
Lansdowne Prize for Poetry/Prix Lansdowne de poésie.
She has previously served as the Manitoba rep for the
League of Canadian Poets and currently sits as secretary
on the League's National Council.

NOTES AND ACKNOWLEDGMENTS

Always to my husband Todd Besant without whose support and unflinching honesty, I might flounder.

Laura Lush was a perfect editor with a light, astute touch and a poetic mind that so easily understood my own.

Versions of Caritas, Sagitarius A*, and Memories of Dystopian Home appeared in *Prairie Fire*.

I am grateful to my cat Dante for the verbatim text of the poem Utilitarianism: as written by cat, though I provided the sonnet-like line breaks.

A nod to Debra Mosher: something you said in 2001 that I carried all these years and finally used in this book.

Close Throat is an ekphrastic poem in response to a collage-art installation by Bonnie Marin called "What are you scared of?" at The University of Manitoba School of Art Gallery in 2013.

A valuable resource was: *The Happiness Hypothesis: Finding Modern Truth in Ancient Wisdom*, Jonathan Haidt, Basic Books, 2006.

Crying: Discussing its Critical Steps was erased from the research paper: Crying: discussing its basic reasons and uses, Maria Miceli, Cristiano Castelfranchi, *New Ideas in Psychology* 21 (2003) 247–273

Erasing the music garden was erased from poem Music Garden from *Music Garden*, Jim Nason, Frontenac House, 2013.

Sources for the equations and models:

Eight Domains of the Canadian Index of Wellbeing https://uwaterloo.ca/canadian-index-wellbeing;

Happiness Economics definition: https://en.wikipedia.org/wiki/Happiness_economics;

Gross National Happiness http://www.grossnationalhappiness.com/;

Happiness = P + (5xE) + (3xH) http://edition.cnn.com/2003/WORLD/europe/01/06/happiness.equation/;

Happy Planet Index http://www.happyplanetindex.org;

Human Development Index http://www.un.org/popin/regional/asiapac/fiji/news/97jun/1page697.htm;

Human Poverty Index http://www.un.org/popin/regional/asiapac/fiji/news/97jun/1page697.htm;

Momentary Subjective Well-Being A computational and neural model of momentary subjective well-being. Rutledge RB, Skandali N, Dayan P, Dolan RJ. Proc Natl Acad Sci USA. 2014 Aug 19;111(33):12252-7;

The Popsicle Index The Popsicle Index is a quality of life measurement coined by Catherine Austin Fitts;

Positive and Negative Affect Schedule (PANAS) Watson, D., Clark, L. A., & Tellegen, A. (1988). Development and validation of brief measures of positive and negative affect: The PANAS scales. Journal of Psychology, 54(6), 1063-1070;

The World Happiness Report http://worldhappiness.report/; Wit = α + βxit + εit. Wit = α + βxit + εit is a standard microeconometric happiness equation;

Where-to-Be-Born Index http://www.eiu.com/